Extracting the Precious From
Nehemiah

Bethany House Books
by Donna Partow

EXTRACTING THE PRECIOUS
A BIBLE STUDY FOR WOMEN

Extracting the Precious From

Nehemiah

Donna Partow

with Lin Johnson

BETHANYHOUSE
Minneapolis, Minnesota

DONNA PARTOW is a Christian communicator with a compelling testimony of God's transforming power. Her uncommon transparency and passion for Christ have been used by God at women's conferences and retreats throughout North America. She is the bestselling author of numerous books and has been a popular guest on hundreds of radio and TV programs, including *Focus on the Family.*

If your church sponsors an annual women's conference or retreat, perhaps they would be interested in learning more about the author's special weekend programs. For more information, contact:

Donna Partow
Web site: *www.donnapartow.com*
E-mail: donnapartow@cox.net

LIN JOHNSON is managing editor of *The Christian Communicator, Advanced Christian Writer,* and *Church Libraries.* She has written over sixty books, specializing in Bible curriculum, and is a Gold Medallion Book Award recipient. Lin directs the Write-to-Publish Conference in the Chicago area and teaches at conferences across the country and internationally. She resides near Chicago. Her Web site is *www.wordprocommunications.com.*

Contents

Preface

EXTRACTING THE PRECIOUS
Bible Study Series

This Bible study series began the day it finally dawned on me that there were two ways to learn the life lessons God has in store for us: the easy way and the hard way. Personally, I've always specialized in learning my lessons the hard way, through painful life experiences. Sure, I've learned a lot, but I've got the battle scars to prove it too. The easy way to learn is sitting at the feet of Jesus, meditating upon His Word. The longer I walk with God, the more determined I become to learn directly from Him—sitting quietly in the privacy of my prayer room rather than learning as I get jostled around out there in the cold, cruel world. Which way would you rather learn?

I used to think I was "getting away with something" when I neglected the spiritual disciplines such as prayer, Bible study, Scripture memorization, and participating in a small group study. But I was only deceiving myself. The plain and simple fact is this: We all reap what we sow. Nothing more, nothing less. God won't force you to study your Bible. He won't come down from heaven and clobber you over the head if you skip some of the questions in this book. He won't even be mad at you if you put this down right now and never pick it up again. In fact, God will love you the exact same amount. His unfailing love for you is completely unconditional.

But God's love doesn't wipe out the logical consequences of our choices. Here's how Deuteronomy 30:19–20 puts it:

*This day I call heaven and earth as witnesses against
you that I have set before you life and death, blessings and
curses. Now choose life, so that you and your children may
live and that you may love the Lord your God, listen to his
voice, and hold fast to him.*

Reading God's Word is the ultimate choice for life, not only for
us but to those who will come after us. Every moment we choose
to spend searching, meditating, memorizing is a choice for life.
Every moment we neglect His Word, we are choosing death—the
death of our spiritual and personal potential; the death of an opportunity to become all God desires us to be. God's love is unconditional, but His blessings are not. Here's how the psalmist put it:

*Blessed is the man
who does not walk in the counsel of the wicked
or stand in the way of sinners
or sit in the seat of mockers.
But his delight is in the law of the Lord,
and on his law he meditates day and night.
He is like a tree planted by streams of water,
which yields its fruit in season
and whose leaf does not wither.
Whatever he does prospers.*

—Psalm 1:1–3

God says we will be blessed (happy, fortunate, prosperous, and
enviable) if we spend more time in His Word and less time with
clueless people (my paraphrase). Does that mean we'll never have
to learn anything the hard way? Not quite! Let's face it: Certain clas-
ses require a "hands-on" component. I couldn't graduate from
chemistry class without stepping into the lab, putting on my scien-
tist-wanna-be (or in my case, scientist-never-gonna-be) coat, and
conducting some of those experiments for myself. At the same time,
I found that my ability to conduct those experiments successfully
was directly linked to the amount of time I spent studying the text-
book in advance. You can't learn what it is to be a parent without

having children underfoot. Neither can you fully comprehend God's faithfulness without finding yourself trapped in the middle of a real-world situation where nothing else can see you through. Nevertheless, there is much we *can* learn in solitude and study of God's Word so when we encounter various tests in life, we'll be well-prepared to experience a successful outcome.

Jeremiah 15:19 is a passage that has always been especially meaningful to me:

> *Therefore, thus says the Lord,*
> *"If you return, then I will restore you—*
> *Before Me you will stand;*
> *And if you extract the precious from the worthless,*
> *You will become My spokesman."*
> *—Jeremiah 15:19* NASB

The first time I heard those words, my heart leapt within me and I said, "Yes, Lord, I want to extract the precious from every worthless circumstance I must endure!" I was instantly overtaken with a holy determination to learn all I could from every class I landed in at the School of Hard Knocks.

Those of you who are familiar with my work know I've built my writing and speaking ministry on story illustrations and life lessons gleaned from my various follies and foibles. My friends all tease me whenever they see me embroiled in yet another mess, "Don't worry, Donna. You'll get through this . . . and turn it into a great illustration." And they're right! I always do. But with this new series, I wanted to do something entirely different. I wanted my readers to know that just as we can extract the precious from the worthless, we can extract the precious from the precious too! Rather than telling you my stories, I wanted you to read His story. You can learn to glean story illustrations and life lessons while sitting peacefully at His feet rather than getting bloodied out in the street. Isn't that a beautiful thought?

The other thing I wanted to share with you is this: I love learning from other people, but I'd much rather learn from God. As much as I enjoy reading Christian books, completing various Bible studies, listening to teaching tapes, and attending conferences, nothing on earth compares to those moments when I realize God has cut out the middleman. When it's just Him, His Word, and me, He is serving as my personal tutor. That's when His Word truly comes alive for me. And that's what I want you to experience for yourself with the EXTRACTING THE PRECIOUS studies. I want to get out of the way as much as possible and let God teach you directly from His Word. You'll notice that I've saved my pithy little comments for the end of each chapter, so you aren't biased by my perspective on what's important. You can decide that for yourself.

USING THIS STUDY GUIDE

Every book in this series will feature twelve chapters, each of which is divided into three sections:

Search the Word features a series of inductive Bible study questions designed to help you interact with the Bible text. Use a Bible version that is easy to understand. I recommend the New International Version, but if you prefer a different version (e.g., New King James, New American Standard, *New Living*), that's fine. You may enjoy reading from several translations, and if you're a true scholar, the *Amplified Bible* is ideal for studying a passage in depth. You may want to complete each study in two or three sittings rather than answering all the questions at once. Then, instead of simply copying the Bible text, answer the questions in your own words.

Consider the Message provides a narrative section that illustrates the truth of the chapter, showing how it can be lived out in today's world.

Apply the Truth contains questions to help you apply the biblical teaching to your daily life, along with a verse or short passage to memorize. Depend on the Holy Spirit to guide and help you with these questions so He can pinpoint areas of your life where God wants you to practice His truth.

Although I suspect many of you will be using these books for your personal quiet time, I have included a brief Leader's Guide at the end of each book. It includes some background information on the Bible text, along with cross-references and suggestions for using this study guide in a group setting.

I want you to know how excited I am for you as you begin this journey with God and His Word. You will soon discover (if you don't know this already) that the truths you glean on your own will ultimately have far greater impact on your life than anything you've ever learned secondhand. People died to give us the right to study God's Word for ourselves. It's a great privilege. Make the most of it. As you do, here's my prayer for you:

> For this reason I kneel before the Father, from whom
> his whole family in heaven and on earth derives its name.
> I pray that out of his glorious riches he may strengthen you
> with power through his Spirit in your inner being, so that
> Christ may dwell in your hearts through faith. And I pray
> that you, being rooted and established in love, may have
> power, together with all the saints, to grasp how wide and
> long and high and deep is the love of Christ, and to know
> this love that surpasses knowledge—that you may be filled
> to the measure of all the fullness of God.
>
> Now to him who is able to do immeasurably more than
> all we ask or imagine, according to his power that is at
> work within us, to him be glory in the church and in Christ
> Jesus throughout all generations, for ever and ever! Amen.
> —Ephesians 3:14–21

Blessings,
His Vessel
Donna Partow

Introduction

When It's Time to Rebuild

The book of Nehemiah led me on a journey to the greatest personal revival I've ever experienced. As I've read this book over and over, witnessing the powerful impact of confession, repentance, and obedience, it has taken me back to basics. It took me back to the foundations of faith, challenging me to rebuild in the areas of personal and spiritual discipline. It challenged me to build with the bricks already at my disposal: prayer, fasting, and the study of God's Word. It reminded me that God wants us to learn from those faithful men and women who've gone before us. They left an example for a reason: so we can follow in their footsteps. I can honestly say that there were moments as I wrote this book when I felt closer to God than I have ever been.

As I've shared insights from this book with my weekly women's Bible study, I've seen tremendous growth in their lives. Revival is breaking out in our midst! Lives are being radically changed, not through some "new" discovery, but through old truths. Old truths, such as confession, must lead to genuine repentance. It's not enough to be sorry for our sin; we have to change the way we live. The problem isn't everyone else's sin; the problem isn't even opposition from the enemy (although we had better learn to expect it). The problem is our own hardened hearts. Repentance alone can lead to revival. As we return to God and rebuild the foundations of our faith, revival will overflow in spontaneous joy. I know, because lately I can't stop singing, even though I can't carry a tune!

THE STORY BEHIND NEHEMIAH

Nehemiah is a powerful book because Nehemiah's life sets a powerful example. As the chapters progress, we watch him work his way through three different job assignments: from cupbearer to a pagan king; to general contractor for a massive reconstruction project; to governor; back to cupbearer; and, finally, to governor again. Through all these challenges and changes, one thing remains the same: Nehemiah's integrity. Whatever he finds to do, he does it with all his heart and he does it as though God himself were his employer.

Nehemiah was both a thoughtful man of prayer and a passionate man of action—a rare combination. He must have been exceptionally trustworthy to secure a position as cupbearer to Artexerxes I, the king of Persia. When he heard that the walls of Jerusalem had crumbled, he didn't take rash action, didn't try to take matters into his own hands. Instead, he devoted himself to prayer and fasting, quietly waiting for God to move the heart of the king. But once he saw that God was at work, he did not hesitate to make bold requests for assistance from Artexerxes. Nehemiah not only recognized the problem, he was willing to be part of the solution, even though it meant uprooting his entire life and walking away from an influential government position to live in a dangerous city.

Even though the book of Nehemiah appears in the first half of the Old Testament in our Bibles, it—along with Ezra and Esther—records events from the end of Old Testament history, starting in 445 B.C. Almost 150 years earlier, the Babylonians had captured the southern kingdom of Judah. Even though God allowed this captivity as judgment for the Israelites' disobedience (1 Kings 9:1–9), He also promised to restore them to their land (Jeremiah 25:11).

After the Persians overthrew the Babylonians, they allowed the Jewish exiles to return to their land. The people went back in three groups. First, in 538 B.C., about forty to fifty thousand Jews returned under Zerubbabel's leadership (Ezra 1–6). With aid from King Darius of Persia, they were able to rebuild the temple, which was completed in 515 B.C. In 479 B.C., Esther became queen of Persia and thwarted an evil plan to destroy the Jewish people. About twenty years later (458 B.C.), Ezra led the second expedition of about five thousand people to Jerusalem (Ezra 7–10). Although they accomplished some good, fourteen years passed with no progress made on rebuilding the city wall.

That's where the story of Nehemiah begins. When he learned that the walls had not been rebuilt, he was alarmed. He knew that a city without walls is an open invitation for enemy invasion. The Bible says, "Like a city whose walls are broken down is a man who lacks self-control" (Proverbs 25:28).

Today, people are self-consumed rather than self-controlled. Our walls are broken down, and the result is broken relationships, broken families, broken churches, broken morality, and a broken society.

It's time to rebuild. If you are ready to set to work on your portion of the wall, join me in this study as we discover principles from Nehemiah's life that can make a difference in our lives today.

Session One
Nehemiah 1

Rebuilding Is Rooted in Prayer

SEARCH THE WORD

1 What is your first reaction when you get bad news?

Why?

Nehemiah's reaction to bad news, as recorded in chapter 1, gives us an excellent example to follow.

Read verses 1-3.

2 What was Nehemiah concerned about?

Why?

3 What report did he get from Hanani and the men of Judah?

4 What circumstances does the phrase "in great trouble and disgrace" (v. 3) convey?

Read verses 4-11.

5 How did Nehemiah react to their report?

6 Why did their report cause Nehemiah to mourn?

Communion with God will best prepare us for our dealings with men. When we have entrusted our concerns to God, the mind is set at liberty; it feels satisfaction and composure, and difficulties vanish. We know that if the affair be hurtful, he can easily hinder it; and if it be good for us, he can as easily forward it.

–matthew henry

7 What do you learn about God from the way Nehemiah addressed Him in his prayer?

8 What did Nehemiah confess to God? Why?

9 What command did Nehemiah remind God of? Why?

10 How did Nehemiah describe God's people?

11 What requests did Nehemiah make?

12 How do you know Nehemiah expected God to answer his prayer?

13 Based on this chapter, what kind of man was Nehemiah?

> **Give me one hundred preachers who fear nothing but sin, and desire nothing but God, and I care not a straw whether they be clergymen or laymen; such alone will shake the gates of hell and set up the kingdom of heaven on earth. God does nothing but in answer to prayer.**
> –john wesLey

CONSIDER THE MESSAGE

I've had the privilege of speaking at women's conferences and retreats all over North America. In the process, hopefully I've learned a thing or two about how God works in the world. If I were to sum it up in one sentence, I'd say: When it comes to accomplishing Kingdom work, given the choice between fifty women who are willing to work hard or one woman who knows how to pray, I'd choose the one woman any day.

> It may be put down as a spiritual axiom that in every truly successful ministry prayer is an evident and controlling force—evident and controlling in the life of the preacher, evident and controlling in the deep spirituality of his work. A ministry may be a very thoughtful ministry without prayer; the preacher may secure fame and popularity without prayer; the whole machinery of the preacher's life and work may be run without the oil of prayer or with scarcely enough to grease one cog; but no ministry can be a spiritual one, securing holiness in the preacher and in his people, without prayer being made an evident and controlling force.
>
> —e. m. bounds

This past summer, my home church hosted a five-week series based on my recent book, *This Isn't the Life I Signed Up For . . . But I'm Finding Hope and Healing.* We didn't have time to recruit a large team of women and didn't have time for adequate preparations. Instead, a handful of women gathered for prayer every week for two months. Yes, we tended to logistics and did a fair amount of roll-up-your-sleeves work. But primarily, we prayed. And God moved. Our original goal was for seventy-five to a hundred women. God had other ideas; more than nine hundred women attended.

My husband's favorite verse is Luke 15:31: "'My son . . . you are always with me, and everything I have is yours.'" God's resources are truly unlimited. Everything God has is at our disposal if only we ask according to His will. God has been reminding me of that fact day and night for the past week, as the leaders of the Christian school my children attend called a meeting to discuss its dire financial straits. An amazing peace settled over the room as the realization collectively dawned that God could *very easily* provide every penny the school needs—and a million dollars more. All we have to do is *ask* and believe that, as we are faithful to carry out God's purposes, God will provide the resources.

Nehemiah understood this truth well. He knew God could move the heart and hands—not only of the faithful but also of a pagan king. God can provide for his children *any way He wants to*. He is the God of the universe, not just God of the church.

When Nehemiah learned that the people of God were in dire straits, he didn't spring into action or try to take matters into his own hands. Nor did he surrender to despair, declaring the situation a hopeless cause. Instead, he immediately entered into a time of mourning, fasting, and prayer. Is that how we respond when we hear the needs of God's people, whether they are at our church or across the globe? It should be. I believe Nehemiah models a way of life that should characterize all believers: a personal connection with God and a passionate concern for the people of God.

The opening chapter of Nehemiah also provides a model of prayer, which if we were to master it would render all books and seminars on prayer obsolete. The first thing I notice is that Nehemiah's prayers are rooted in an awareness of both God's character and God's promises. He acknowledges not only God's position as ruler but his nature as a covenant-maker and covenant-keeper (v. 5). Next, Nehemiah confesses both personal and national sins (vv. 6–7). Then he bases his request on principles and promises set forth in God's Word (vv. 8–9). This vital ingredient is essential to all true prayer.

Then, and only then, does Nehemiah make his request known (v. 11). I love the fact that his prayer is specific and bold, without being outcome-based. Too often we tell God exactly what we want to see happen, and how and when we want it to unfold. Nehemiah doesn't do that. Instead, he simply says, "God, I want you to grant me favor in the eyes of this man. I don't know what that will look like or what the exact outcome will be, but I know that's what I need."

As we shall see in the next chapter, the outcome is above and beyond what Nehemiah might have asked at this moment. It's a lesson to all of us who desire to learn how to pray effectually: Ask God for what we need (which is simply the opportunity to advance His purposes), but let Him handle the details involved in bringing it to pass.

APPLY THE TRUTH

1 How do your prayers compare with Nehemiah's?

2 What changes do you want to make in your prayer life this week to follow his example?

3 Memorize Nehemiah 1:11:

> **O Lord, let your ear be attentive to the prayer of this your servant and to the prayer of your servants who delight in revering your name.**

Session Two
Nehemiah 2

Rebuilding Takes Preparation

SEARCH THE WORD

1 When you want to do a job, how much preparation do you do before starting it?

Why?

Nehemiah was a man who knew the value of preparation before beginning a job, as he demonstrated in chapter 2.

Read verses 1–10.

2 Why did Nehemiah have access to the king?

> Faith is not a synonym for disorder or a substitute for careful planning.
> –chuck swindoLL

3 Why was Nehemiah sad?

4 How did his sadness catch the king's attention?

> **Nehemiah had not only prayed and sought God's help but he used all of the human resources that were available—including his intellectual skills, his human experiences, his accumulated wisdom, his role and position, and the people with whom he came in contact.**
>
> —gene a. getz

5 How did Nehemiah integrate his faith with this audience before the king?

6 What was different about Nehemiah's prayer here and the one recorded in chapter 1?

7 What did Nehemiah request in preparation for rebuilding the walls of Jerusalem?

8 On a scale of 1 to 10, how audacious were Nehemiah's requests?

Why?

9 Why did the king grant Nehemiah's requests?

10 How can you tell when "the good hand" of your God is on you?

Read verses 11–16.

11 Why do you think Nehemiah didn't tell anyone why he was in Jerusalem?

12 How did Nehemiah prepare for rebuilding the walls?

Read verses 17–20.

13 How did Nehemiah "sell" his project of rebuilding the walls?

14 How did the people respond?

15 How did Nehemiah deal with detractors?

> **For many people, opposition raises serious doubts about whether we're in God's will. In Nehemiah's case the opposition of those who despised the things of God served as an affirmation that he *was* doing God's will.**
> –chuck swindoLL

16 What gave Nehemiah his confidence in this situation?

CONSIDER THE MESSAGE

This chapter of Nehemiah is like a crash course on ministry preparation. Since I believe every Christian is handpicked by God for a specific purpose and that we each have a Kingdom assignment to fulfill, it's vitally important to grab hold of the principles set forth here. I notice at least seven.

First, all true ministry begins in God's heart. We can stay busy our entire lives doing church work, but authentic transformation—of an individual, a church, or a society—always flows down from above. So Nehemiah's work began much earlier, as recorded in verse

12: "What my God had put in my heart to do." This wasn't something Nehemiah decided to do *for God;* this was something God wanted to do *through Nehemiah.* See the difference? Forget about the people who are trying to recruit you for this, that, or the other program at church. What has *God* laid on your heart? You cannot even begin to prepare until you start there.

Second, we see the importance of a quiet season of preparation before entering into ministry. Nehemiah spent time in prayer and fasting, seeking God's perspective and wisdom before doing anything else. Too often people who feel called to ministry think they need to start immediately. That's rarely the case. In fact, it's not unusual for an extended period of time to pass. For Moses, it was forty years; David waited fifteen before ascending to the throne. In my own life, seventeen years transpired after the night I clearly heard God call me into ministry before I began speaking at women's retreats. So Nehemiah's silent season of four months was relatively brief, maybe because he was such a quick learner.

Third, preparation begins with prayer, but it doesn't stop there. When Nehemiah finally had the opportunity to make his request known to King Artaxerxes, it's obvious he had thought through *and* planned out almost every detail. When you begin your preparations in prayer, God will bring things to your attention that you might have missed otherwise. As a result, you'll be more efficient. We're foolish to think we can save time by rushing forward, rather than taking time to sit at His feet. Imagine, for example, if Nehemiah had dashed off *without* those letters granting him safe passage. He might have been killed or, at the very least, forced to turn back and start the trip all over again. Whenever I pray for an upcoming project, I always keep pen and paper handy. Inevitably, God starts communicating a detailed plan of action to me.

Something tells me Nehemiah took notes when he was praying. When the king questioned him, he was able to provide a time frame, had thought about possible obstacles (e.g., passing through potentially hostile territory) and key players/decision makers who could help him overcome those obstacles (governors), and had determined what resources (timber) he would need and who could supply them (Asaph). Whew! The one thing he apparently didn't ask for was also provided: army captains and the cavalry.

Fourth, you can be bold when you've spent time with God and are confident you've heard from Him. Nehemiah not only asked for supplies to rebuild the temple and the city wall but for his own residence as well. This request may seem selfish or presumptuous, but it's not. Some people (namely people who are *not* in ministry) think everyone in ministry should live like John the Baptist, eating locusts out in the desert. While we shouldn't be greedy, there's nothing wrong with asking that our basic needs be met. Nehemiah obviously felt he'd be a better leader living in a house rather than sleeping in a tent (perhaps because he would be better rested?). God knows what *you* need to minister effectively, and He's willing to provide it. But you may still have to ask those who are in a position to help you for their assistance.

Fifth, Nehemiah knew that "only fools rush in." It's tempting, when we get excited about something God has called us to do, to conduct ourselves like the proverbial bull in a china shop. As a result, we leave a trail of offended people behind us. On arriving in Jerusalem, Nehemiah continued to act thoughtfully and prayerfully, taking three more days to fully evaluate the situation. He didn't operate like the Lone Ranger. He had a core of key supporters who inspected the damage with him; then he recruited a whole army of volunteers. I also appreciate the fact that Nehemiah gave people credit for being able to recognize the problem for themselves. He doesn't come across as the "all-insightful one," but rather only one among many who saw the grave condition the Israelites were in.

Sixth, Nehemiah quickly discovered that rebuilding, even with God as the architect, doesn't mean you won't face opposition. But when you have prayed, prepared, and recruited others, you'll have the courage of your convictions and the strength to keep going in the face of ridicule.

Finally, Nehemiah knew his planning wasn't enough. He publicly acknowledged that it was only because of the gracious hand of God upon him that anything of Kingdom value could be accomplished. The truth is, you can be the most qualified, well-prepared person on the planet, but if God doesn't grant you favor and His hand is not upon you, it is all in vain.

APPLY THE TRUTH

1 How can you follow Nehemiah's example of preparation the next time you tackle a job or project?

2 How can you demonstrate the same kind of God-confidence Nehemiah had in the face of opposition to a job or project?

3 Memorize Nehemiah 2:8:

> **And because the gracious hand of my God
> was upon me, the king granted my requests.**

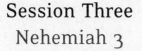

Session Three
Nehemiah 3

Rebuilding Requires Teamwork

SEARCH THE WORD

1 Describe a time when you were part of a ministry or work team.

What did you enjoy about being on that team?

Nehemiah knew the value of teamwork, as he demonstrated in chapter 3.

No one can whistle a symphony. It takes an orchestra to play it.
−halford e. luccock

Read verses 1-32.

2 How did Nehemiah accomplish the work of rebuilding the wall?

3 How did the priests set an example for the rest of the people on this team?

4 What do you learn about the people involved in rebuilding the walls and repairing the gates?

5 Why were the people motivated to do this work?

It marks a big step in a man's development when he comes to realize that other men can be called in to help him do a better job than he can do alone.
–andrew carnegie

6 Who refused to be part of this work team (v. 5)?

7 Why do you think they refused to help?

8 How can you keep from having the same attitude the next time you're invited to be part of a work team?

9 Although most of the team was composed of men, what part did women play (v. 12)?

10 What impresses you most about Nehemiah's plan to rebuild the walls and repair the gates?

12 What does the detail in this chapter tell you about Nehemiah?

13 What do you learn about God from the details recorded in this chapter?

CONSIDER THE MESSAGE

I'll never forget the Sunday morning when my pastor, Dr. Gary Kinnamen, "nailed" me with a powerful illustration. He said, "Some people live the Christian life as if it were a chess game they can play solo. They buy the chess board and a stack of books. Then they sit at home alone, studying, pondering, moving their pawns. But they never engage in a real match. If your entire Christian experience consists of you and God, you're out of balance. And, what's worse, you are deceiving yourself because you think you're serving and pleasing God; but you're really not."

Ouch.

As we've seen through Nehemiah's example, there's a time for quiet contemplation—for moments between a believer and his or her true King. (That's the part I love!) But preparation for life isn't living. At some point, you have to get in the game. You have to go out into the big, scary world filled with other people. (That's the part I dread!) There's a time to pray, and there's a time to roll up your sleeves and get to work. (Yes, you can pray and work at the *same time*.)

Isn't it incredible that the first person mentioned in verse 1 is the high priest, the top spiritual leader in Israel? He wasn't sitting in his private study somewhere preparing next week's sermon. Instead, he "and his fellow priests went to work and rebuilt the Sheep Gate." Yes indeed, manual labor. In contrast, there were big shots (the nobles) who wouldn't put their shoulders to the work. There are many senior pastors and other prominent Christians today who would consider such work beneath them. Some things never change.

I know from personal experience how tempting it is to say, "Well, my gift is teaching, so I never have to meet anyone's practical needs." Of course, God wants us to exercise our gifts; He doesn't want the mouth in the body of Christ trying to function like a foot. But it's easy to hide behind our spiritual gifts, using them as excuses to avoid the more mundane, unpleasant tasks required to keep every church going. Guess what? You don't need the spiritual gift of cleaning to vacuum the church nursery. What a revelation!

Lately, Dr. Kinnamen has been challenging our congregation to begin volunteering to *serve* our community. (Notice, he didn't say become leaders—he said *servants.*) For too long, many American Christians have thought our only civic responsibility was voting for people who professed to share our family values. We thought our only obligation to the world around us was to deliver mini-sermons to our unsaved friends and neighbors. But when the walls are crumbling all around us, as they are in this country today, it's time to get to work.

Even though our pastor leads a congregation of several thousand, he's not hiding in his office. Instead, every Thursday morning he works at a local food pantry, hoping that others will follow his example. It's time for the church to take up the towel and begin serving people, rather than trying to straighten them out. It's our job to love our neighbors in practical ways and leave the straightening out to God.

> **Our main business is not to see what lies dimly at a distance, but to do what lies clearly at hand.**
> –thomas carlyle

One of the most beautiful aspects of real-world Christian servanthood is that it brings you shoulder to shoulder with people you would otherwise never encounter. Scanning the chapter, you'll notice goldsmiths, perfume makers, merchants, and priests working side by side. These are people with little in common, who probably wouldn't socialize with one another. But because they were all focused on the larger purpose, suddenly their common cause was more significant than their differences.

Woven into the catalog of wall repairers are two that caught my attention. Verse 20 tells us that "Baruch son of Zabbai zealously repaired another section." Virtually the entire nation was rebuilding the wall, but something about his enthusiasm was noteworthy. My guess is that it was contagious!

Backing up a few verses (v. 12), Nehemiah mentioned that Shallum worked "with the help of his daughters." You get the feeling that something special happened in that family as they labored side by side. Recently, the women's ministry director at my church introduced me to her teenage daughter. I had been wanting to meet her because I prayed for the two of them last summer when they went to Guatemala together as part of a work team. This mother-daughter pair were smiling ear to ear as they shared that nothing has brought them closer together than serving God side by side.

Servanthood and teamwork make the perfect combination. And

the best place to start is where the Israelites began—right outside your own front door.

APPLY THE TRUTH

1 What keeps you from asking for help when you're working in a ministry or on a project for your church or another group?

2 What steps can you take this week to utilize more teamwork in your church or small group?

3 How can you be a better team member in your current ministry or a future one?

4 Memorize Nehemiah 3:28:

> **The priests made repairs, each in front of his own house.**

Session Four
Nehemiah 4

Rebuilding Invites Opposition

SEARCH THE WORD

1 What's your first reaction when someone opposes you or a project you're working on?

Why?

Nehemiah faced a lot of opposition while he led the Jewish people to rebuild the wall around Jerusalem. Notice how he reacted to it as you study chapter 4.

Read verses 1-3.

2 How did Sanballat and Tobiah respond to the rebuilding of the wall?

Why?

Read verses 4-5.

3 In response to Sanballat and Tobiah, what did Nehemiah pray?

> **Opposition is not only an evidence that God is blessing, but it is also an opportunity for us to grow.... "God had one Son without sin," said Charles Spurgeon, "but He never had a son without a trial."**
> –warren w. wiersbe

4 How could he ask God not to forgive them?

Read verses 6-15.

5 How did the people's attitude affect the rebuilding project?

6 When have you seen your church or study group work "with all their heart"?

7 What new threats did the people face as they rebuilt the wall?

> **The more we study Scripture, the more we see that prayer alone is seldom God's plan for us when we face difficulties. God grants us the privilege to pray about *everything* but He also expects us to do *everything* we can to resolve our problems.**
>
> —gene a. getz

8 How did some of the people's attitudes feed into that opposition?

9 How did Nehemiah handle these new threats?

> **Nehemiah wisely directed the attention of the discouraged wall builders from their overwhelming opposition to their omnipotent Lord! A proper view of God puts all difficulties in right perspective.**
>
> —j. karL Laney

Read verses 16–23.

10 What was Nehemiah's solution for proceeding with the work?

11 How did Nehemiah express his confidence in finishing this project?

12 What example did Nehemiah set for the people?

CONSIDER THE MESSAGE

My neighborhood is 90 percent Mormon, if you can imagine that. Mormons' lives are fascinating to watch: The women never gain weight, even after giving birth to eight kids. Their church tells them, "You should take care of your body. Don't drink caffeine or eat junk food again." And they all exclaim, "Okay," and spend the rest of their lives eating freshly ground whole wheat bread and tofu casseroles—and the entire family is *grateful* for that food. The teenagers are all exceptionally good-looking and blemish-free. They get excellent grades and stay out of trouble. Just this morning, I observed that Mormons' lawns never even seem to sprout any weeds.

Okay, I'm exaggerating a tad. But it's quite remarkable how well their lives "work." Frankly, it used to bug me. Here I am with my sound biblical doctrine, yet my life feels like a war zone. I was sharing my frustration with Candy Davison, director of women's ministries at Sandy Cove Conference Center. Unmoved by my litany of impressive Mormon achievements, she remarked, "The explanation is easy. They don't have an Enemy."

Wow! That was the answer. So I got to thinking about how we, as Christians, could tap into this power the Mormons have laid hold of. Here's my brilliant-beyond-brilliant idea for how you, too, can have a comfortable, well-ordered life.

Are you ready for my surefire plan for keeping the devil off your back? (Drum roll, please!) Don't do anything for the Kingdom of God. Devote yourself entirely to selfish pursuits. Refuse to care about anyone on the planet other than your immediate family and circle of friends. Trust me, this lifestyle will work. Not only will the devil leave you alone, he'll go out of his way to help you. I once heard it said, "The devil is never too busy to rock the cradle of a sleeping saint."

There are Christians like this in every church. They never have any major problems, so they congratulate themselves on making Christianity "work" for them. But that's not the issue. The issue is: Are *you* working for Christianity? We're not supposed to be following God for what we can get, but for what we've already gotten: mercy at the foot of the Cross. If the devil isn't opposing you, guess what? There's only one explanation. It's because you're not doing anything to oppose, so he is content to let you keep napping.

> **Work as if everything depended upon your work, and pray as if everything depended upon your prayer.**
>
> –general william booth

Opposition is actually good news. It means you are doing something worthwhile, and the devil is pitching a fit over it. I finally realized that the reason my life feels like a war is because Christians who want their lives to count for the Kingdom are, in fact, on the front line of a war. So you've got a decision to make: Do you want your life to be comfortable, or do you want your life to count?

In chapter 4, we see that Nehemiah faced constant opposition. And the more obvious it became that his work was effective, the more intense the pressure mounted against him. First the enemy ridiculed and tried to discourage him. Then he tried to stir people up against Nehemiah. When that didn't work, he turned up the heat by using intimidation.

But Nehemiah was undeterred, so he did not for one minute let the enemy distract him from the task. The devil loves to distract people who are about the Lord's business! Don't fall for this tactic. Be as steadfast as Nehemiah, who prayed that God would handle his enemies. He refused to give way to fear, instead trusting God's awesome power.

Yet, while he relied on God, Nehemiah also armed all the people, who worked with one hand and held a weapon in the other. Let's not be naïve, but balanced. Verse 9 sums it up perfectly: "But we prayed to our God *and* posted a guard day and night to meet this threat" (emphasis added). When it comes to advancing God's purposes on earth, we need both the power of God to defeat the enemy and the sweat of fearless men and women willing to join the battle.

APPLY THE TRUTH

1 What kinds of opposition do you face personally or in your ministry?

2 What have you learned from Nehemiah's strategy for opposition that will help you the next time you face some?

3 Memorize Nehemiah 4:9:

> **But we prayed to our God and posted a**
> **guard day and night to meet this threat.**

Session Five
Nehemiah 5

Rebuilding Develops Compassion for Others

SEARCH THE WORD

1 Given the opportunity to make a lot of money or help others, which would you typically choose?

Why?

If we're honest, most of us tend to be far more selfish than compassionate. And we're not alone, as Nehemiah chapter 5 demonstrates.

Read verses 1–5.

2 What new kinds of opposition did Nehemiah have to deal with from his own people?

3 Who were the people responsible for those problems?

4 Why would they act like this?

Read verses 6–13.

5 Why was Nehemiah angry about the nobles' and officials' lack of compassion?

> To consider persons and events and situations only in the light of their effect upon myself is to live on the doorstep of hell.
> –thomas merton

6 What was his solution for this situation?

7 How did they respond to Nehemiah's request?

8 What did Nehemiah do to guarantee they'd follow through?

Though I speak with the tongues of men and of angels, and have not charity, I am become as sounding brass, or a tinkling cymbal. And though I have the gift of prophecy, and understand all mysteries, and all knowledge; and though I have all faith, so that I could remove mountains, and have not charity, I am nothing. And though I bestow all my goods to feed the poor, and though I give my body to be burned, and have not charity, it profiteth me nothing. Charity suffereth long, and is kind; charity envieth not; charity vaunteth not itself, is not puffed up, doth not behave itself unseemly, seeketh not her own, is not easily provoked, thinketh no evil; rejoiceth not in iniquity, but rejoiceth in the truth; beareth all things, believeth all things, hopeth all things, endureth all things.

Charity never faileth: but whether there be prophecies, they shall fail; whether there be tongues, they shall cease; whether there be knowledge, it shall vanish away. For we know in part, and we prophesy in part. But when that which is perfect is come, then that which is in part shall be done away. When I was a child, I spake as a child, I understood as a child, I thought as a child: but when I became a man, I put away childish things. For now we see through a glass, darkly; but then face to face: now I know in part; but then shall I know even as also I am known. And now abideth faith, hope, charity, these three; but the greatest of these is charity.

—apostle paul (1 corinthians 13 kjv)

9 How did the people support Nehemiah's compassionate action?

Read verses 14-19.

10 How did Nehemiah's behavior differ from that of his predecessors?

Why?

11 Why was Nehemiah's prayer an appropriate accompaniment to his actions?

CONSIDER THE MESSAGE

Whenever I'm studying a passage of Scripture in depth, I look it up in a variety of translations and paraphrases, including the King James Version, The Amplified Bible, and *The Message*. Sometimes reading it from a variety of sources provides greater insight since each rendering has something unique to offer. The Amplified gives a fuller definition, while *The Message* makes the Word fresh and accessible. And every once in a while, the old King James Version just flat-out nails it like no other translation.

Nowhere is that fact more true than in the translation of the

Greek word *agape*. In my humble opinion, to render the word as love is to strip it of all meaning in our contemporary culture, where we love chocolate chip cookies or we love our new car. People engaged in blatant fornication and adultery are said to be making *love*, and those who want to walk away from their commitments claim they've fallen out of love.

The word means less than nothing these days. That's why I love (pun intended) the word *charity*. Perhaps if we put it back in the Bible, Christians might put it back into their lives. It's remarkable to me how few Christians—even those who are earnest students of Scripture—devote any significant amount of time to charity work. Somehow, good doctrine has taken preeminence over goodness itself. Christianity has been reduced to a set of beliefs, something Jesus never intended. Remember the old song "They'll Know We Are Christians by Our Love"? If someone steeped in today's Christian culture were to pen that song, it might go something like this:

> We will talk about the Bible
> We will analyze each word
> We will congratulate ourselves
> On our moral superiority.
> And they'll know we are Christians by our beliefs, by our
>   beliefs.
> Yes, they'll know we are Christians by our beliefs.

Where, oh where, is our compassion for hurting people? Whatever happened to providing practical assistance to those in need? Once upon a time, almost all charities—from soup kitchens to hospitals—were run by earnest Christians who considered serving people the only reasonable response to God's amazing love. When is the last time you personally provided real help—not a sermon or lecture, but real help—to the poor?

I'm not talking about sending money, although that's important. I mean *you* getting up close and personal, face-to-face with the needs of a hurting world that looks something like this:

- 1.3 billion people worldwide live on less than a dollar a day.
- 2.3 billion people drink water contaminated with bacteria and disease.
- 740 million people are severely malnourished.
- 29,000 children die each day of preventable, poverty-related causes.
- 1,200 children die every single hour of every single day. (Statistics courtesy of World Vision)

The people of Nehemiah's day were apparently much like us. They were earnest and devoted to their religion. They had laid down everything else to rebuild the city wall. I don't think they were bad people; they were simply out of touch with the plight of the poor. Once Nehemiah confronted them with a powerful reality check, they were cut to the heart and eager to do what was right.

Of course, Nehemiah also knew that good intentions aren't enough. Again, it wasn't that he didn't trust them. He believed they meant well. But well-meaning and well-doing are often two different things. People who mean well often perform poorly. So Nehemiah held a solemn ceremony to emphasize the seriousness of the commitment they had made to care for the poor. He also pledged to follow up to ensure they followed through. In one of the most beautiful verses of the Bible, we read, "And the people did as they had promised."

> Love can be known only from the actions it prompts.
> –w. e. vine

I would urge you to prayerfully consider the statistics above. Ask God to reveal *your* role in caring for the poor. Perhaps you need to hold a solemn ceremony of your own; or, if you are part of a group, do so together. As a helpful reminder of your commitment, take this challenge: From this day forward, whenever you read the word *love* in your Bible, make a note in the margin: charity.

APPLY THE TRUTH

1 How can you show compassion to people instead of taking advantage of them?

Love is a verb.

   –dc taLk

2 Choose one way to show compassion this week, and write an action plan for doing so.

3 Memorize Nehemiah 5:13:

And the people did as they had promised.

Session Six
Nehemiah 6:1-14

Rebuilding Continues Through Discernment

SEARCH THE WORD

1 When have you been deceived into doing something wrong or sinful?

What happened as a result?

It's so easy to be deceived by people who don't have our best interests at heart. But Nehemiah gives us an example of how to deal with them in chapter 6.

Read verses 1-4.

2 What did Sanballat, Tobiah, and the other enemies want to do after they found out the wall had been rebuilt?

3 How did Nehemiah's response show discernment?

4 What does the number of times they requested an audience with Nehemiah, even though he repeatedly turned them down, tell you about them?

> **Spiritual discernment is a prime need, which nature alone will not supply, and which therefore must be sought from God through godliness as a way and style of life.**
>
> –j. i. packer

Read verses 5-9.

5 After Nehemiah turned down his enemies' invitation four times, how did they try to intimidate him?

6 How would you have reacted to a message like this?

7 How did Nehemiah respond?

Read verses 10-14.

8 What did Shemaiah want Nehemiah to do?

Why?

9 Why do you think he chose the temple for a meeting place?

10 What does Nehemiah's reaction to Shemaiah's advice tell you about Nehemiah?

11 What did Nehemiah discern was his enemies' goal for this new tactic?

12 What do you learn about prayer from Nehemiah?

CONSIDER THE MESSAGE

One thing Nehemiah and I have in common is letters. As a Christian author, I receive many. Most are wonderfully encouraging, but once in a while I get one from someone who feels "called of the Lord" to rip me limb from limb. I'll never forget a letter I received all the way from Portugal from a person who took it upon himself to dissect *Becoming a Vessel God Can Use,* finding fault with every-thing from my grammar to my theology. He closed with, "I look forward to talking with you further." Like I was going to willingly head into the Valley of Oh-No with this guy! Yeah, right.

> **Discernment is God's call to intercession, never to fault finding.**
> –oswaLd chambers

The church today is filled with people who lay claim to the gift of discernment. Often, they are no more than self-appointed critics. As Nehemiah did, it is important for us to discern when someone is truly sent by God and when that person is, in fact, sent by the Enemy to disrupt God's work. From Scripture, we can glean three guidelines for dis-cernment.

First, true discernment is always motivated by love, as we see in Philippians 1:9–11: "And this is my prayer: that your love may abound more and more in knowledge and depth of insight, so that you may be able to discern what is best and may be pure and blameless until the day of Christ, filled with the fruit of righteous-ness that comes through Jesus Christ—to the glory and praise of God."

The result of true discernment is not strife, discord, and a church split; rather, it is the fruit of righteousness. In other words, a person with the gift of spiritual discernment will be characterized by love, joy, peace, patience, kindness, goodness, faithfulness, gen-tleness, and self-control (Galatians 5:22–23). In my experience, self-appointed critics are characterized by harshness, impatience, and a sour expression. They are invariably motivated by envy or judg-ment. Unwilling to look at the plank in their own eye, they become obsessed with the speck in everyone else's eye (Matthew 7:3–5). True discernment grows out of love, not out of a critical spirit.

Second, true discernment is a gift from God. In 1 Kings 3:12, God told Solomon, "I will give you a wise and discerning heart." And as Paul wrote in 1 Corinthians 2:14, "The man without the Spirit does not accept the things that come from the Spirit of God, for they are foolishness to him, and he cannot understand them, because they are spiritually discerned." God's gifts are always given for one purpose: to build up, not tear down, the church. A destructive person is not exercising a gift from God.

In 1 Chronicles 12:22, we learn that "day after day men came to help David, until he had a great army, like the army of God." Among those people God raised up were the "men of Issachar, who understood the times and knew what Israel should do" (v. 32). These men came to help, not to harm. More importantly, they became part of a mighty army. An army works together as the ultimate team. People of true discernment are team players; they are part of the solution. Notice the men of Issachar knew what Israel should *do*, and they were part of the army who got the work done. Self-appointed critics are not team players. They sit on the sidelines, criticizing the people who are actually getting the work done. In short, they are all talk and no action.

> **The credit in life goes not to the critic who stands on the sideline and points out where the strong stumble, but rather, the real credit in life goes to the man who is actually in the arena, whose face may get marred by sweat and dust, who knows great enthusiasm and great devotion and learns to spend himself in a worthy cause, who at best if he wins knows the thrill of high achievement and if he fails, at least fails while daring greatly, so that in life his place will never be with those very cold and timid souls who know neither victory nor defeat.**
> –president theodore roosevelt

Finally, true discernment always gives priority to God's clear, revealed will. Both Nehemiah and the sons of Issachar "knew what Israel should do." They had complete clarity concerning God's calling and purpose. God gave Nehemiah a specific task: rebuilding the wall. Nothing proposed by mere man was enough to drag Nehemiah away from the work assigned to him.

In the Bible, we have the revealed will of God. Our calling and purpose has been made plain: Our love should abound more and more to the praise and glory of his name. Don't get sidetracked by self-appointed critics who want to drag you away from your task into the Valley of Oh-No. Instead, keep rebuilding your section of the wall until the job is done.

APPLY THE TRUTH

1 In what areas do you need to develop more discernment?

2 How can you develop more discernment for the next time someone tries to deceive you?

3 Memorize Nehemiah 6:9:

> **They were all trying to frighten us, thinking, "Their hands will get too weak for the work, and it will not be completed." But I prayed, "Now strengthen my hands."**

Rebuilding Requires Completion

SEARCH THE WORD

1 How often do you complete projects that you start?

What motivates you to finish them? What prevents you from finishing them?

It's not always easy or convenient to finish what we start. But as the people in Nehemiah's day discovered, there are benefits of following through.

Read 6:15-19.

2 What is significant about the fact that it took only fifty-two days to rebuild the wall?

3 What effect did the rebuilding of the wall have on the people's enemies and surrounding nations?

Why?

4 How might the continuing opposition from Tobiah have sidetracked Nehemiah from his God-given task?

Read 7:1-4.

5 What did Nehemiah do after the wall was rebuilt?

6 Why did he choose Hanani and Hananiah to be in charge of Jerusalem?

7 What additional instructions for the people's protection did Nehemiah give Hanani and Hananiah?

Read 7:5–73a.

8 Nehemiah registered the people against the genealogical record he found to determine whether they were of pure Jewish ancestry or not. Why would this be important when repopulating the city?

9 What stands out to you from reading this genealogical record?

> **If God's people don't protect what they have accomplished for the Lord, the enemy will come in and take it over.**
> –warren w. wiersbe

10 Why was it important that the priests could prove their genealogy?

11 Why do you think the registration totals included animals?

12 What does the large amount of contributions recorded in verses 70–72 tell you about the givers?

13 In this seemingly mundane genealogy list, what do you learn about God?

Hard work does not hurt us. We all know what it is to go full speed for long hours, totally involved in an important task. The resulting weariness is matched by a sense of achievement and joy. Not hard work, but doubt and misgiving produce anxiety as we review a month or year and become oppressed by the pile of unfinished tasks.

–charLes e. hummeL

About Nehemiah?

CONSIDER THE MESSAGE

Some of the most powerful words in the book of Nehemiah are contained in this section: "So the wall was completed . . . in fifty-two days" (6:15). And the most important word in that sentence is *completed*.

I have a confession to make: I'm great at starting projects, but I'm not so great at finishing them. I have a feeling I'm not alone. Every January, countless thousands join a local gym determined that *this* is the year they're going to get in shape. My friend Keven Rush, owner of Payson Athletic Club, told me that by mid-February, most of those new members have fallen off the fitness wagon. Just this morning, I heard on the radio that thirty-two million Americans are currently on a low-carb, high-protein diet. In fact, bread sales are plummeting. But how many will stick with it long enough to take off the weight and, more importantly, keep it off? Very few.

The cover of a *New York Times* bestselling diet book proudly claims, "Thousands have already succeeded." That would be great if it weren't for the fact that millions have purchased the book with grand intentions—only to quit before crossing the finish line. The fact that only *thousands* out of those *millions* have succeeded is hardly cause for encouragement.

But it's not only in the area of fitness where we see a great throng of eager-beaver starters and a small number of faithful finishers. See if this scenario sounds familiar. Hidden away in my garage, I have a large plastic bin filled with craft projects in various stages of completion. Some of them have been sitting in there for a decade. Do you have a similar cache? One of my wackiest idiosyncrasies involves painting. No, not landscapes or portraits—just walls. In my last house, there was hardly a room unaffected by my knack for starting paint jobs. For some reason, unknown even to me, I always left a small white patch somewhere: above the kitchen cabinets, behind a bookshelf in the living room, etc. I also had two rooms featuring almost-completely-finished wallpaper borders.

Ready for the twist? My husband declared that he alone would wield the paintbrush in our new house. Well, ten months ago he painted 90 percent of the upstairs hallway. Yes indeed, if you were to come to my house right now, you could easily locate the three undone spots. We're not alone, of course. In his outstanding booklet *Tyranny of the Urgent,* Charles E. Hummel captured the essence of this almost universal human tendency when he wrote, "Unfinished tasks . . . haunt quiet moments."

That's why it's so refreshing when we encounter someone like Nehemiah who actually got the job finished in a timely fashion. Then he went one step further to assure the work wouldn't be undone, by putting men of integrity in charge of protecting it.

I once lived next door to an unfinished house. For the first year or so, it sat completely empty and untended while weeds overtook the yard. Then one day, the family who owned it showed up, announcing their plans to transform the place. They shared their grand vision with me, and I watched with great expectancy the day workmen finally arrived and construction got underway. But since the owners lived three hours away, supervision on the project was lax. The workers sat around most of the day, goofing off, while billing the homeowner extravagant fees. Finally, after laying out a small fortune to a series of irresponsible and incompetent subcontractors, the family decided to move into the ill-conceived, poorly constructed house even though it wasn't completed.

They lasted only six months.

Once again the unfinished house fell vacant. It was such a sad sight to see. Jesus warns us to count the cost before we begin building: "Suppose one of you wants to build a tower. Will he not first sit down and estimate the cost to see if he has enough money to complete it? For if he lays the foundation and is not able to finish it, everyone who sees it will ridicule him, saying, 'This fellow began to build and was not able to finish'" (Luke 14:28–30). The context of this passage is particularly significant. In verse 25, Luke noted "large crowds were traveling with Jesus." Jesus turned to them and said, "Count the cost."

It's easy to get all excited about following Jesus at an evangelistic campaign. It's easy to get excited about serving God when the pastor gives an awesome sermon on a particular topic. You fill out the pledge form, walk down the aisle, sign up as a volunteer, or whatever. But did you count the cost? Are you willing to make the sacrifices necessary to see the job through to completion? That's the real issue.

Gazing on an unfinished house is sad. Watching it become dilapidated is even sadder. But nothing is sadder than gazing on an unfinished life. Or watching a life fall into disrepair because the person wasn't willing to do what needed to be done, when and how it needed to be done.

Starting isn't enough. We must finish the task God has set before us—the task of glorifying Him through our lives. May we all be able to say, along with the Apostle Paul, "I have fought the good fight, I have finished the race, I have kept the faith. Now there is in store for me the crown of righteousness, which the Lord, the righteous Judge, will award to me on that day—and not only to me, but also to all who have longed for his appearing" (2 Timothy 4:7–8).

APPLY THE TRUTH

1 What unfinished tasks, projects, and commitments clutter your life? List them below.

2 Spend time asking God to show you which of these are tasks He wants you to finish, so you can glorify Him. Then cross off everything else on your list. If you get to the other items, fine; if not, it's okay to let them go. But be sure to keep the commitments you've already made.

If the Christian is too busy to stop, take spiritual inventory, and receive his assignments from God, he becomes a slave to the tyranny of the urgent. He may work day and night to achieve much that seems significant to himself and others, but he will not finish the work *God* has for him to do.

–charLes e. hummeL

3 Record an action plan to finish one item left on your list.

4 Memorize Nehemiah 6:15–16:

> **So the wall was completed on the twenty-fifth of Elul, in fifty-two days. When all our enemies heard about this, all the surrounding nations were afraid and lost their self-confidence, because they realized that this work had been done with the help of our God.**

Session Eight
Nehemiah 7:73b–8:18

Rebuilding Unleashes Revival

SEARCH THE WORD

1 How easy is it for you to obey God's Word?

Why?

Most of us struggle with obeying God in at least one area of our lives. But obedience is easier when we understand what He wants us to do and what we'll experience as a result. The Israelites discovered this process after they rebuilt the wall, as recorded in Nehemiah 7:73b–8:18.

Read 7:73b–8:8.

2 What is significant about the people's request of Ezra during the seventh month, *Tishri* (our September/October, which includes Rosh Hashanah and Yom Kippur, holy days that focus on repentance and atonement for sin)?

3 How did the Levites help the people understand what Ezra read to them from the Law?

4 When the people heard the Law and understood what it meant, how did they respond to it?

> **Revival is no more a miracle than a crop of wheat. Revival comes from heaven when heroic souls enter the conflict determined to win or die— or if need be, to win and die! "The kingdom of heaven suffereth violence, and the violent take it by force."**
>
> –charLes q. finney

5 How does your response compare to theirs when you hear God's Word read and taught?

Read 8:9–12.

6 Why didn't Nehemiah and Ezra want the people to continue to mourn and cry as a result of hearing God's Word?

7 What did the people do then in response to understanding God's words?

Read 8:13-18.

> A man never knows joy until he gets rightly related to God.
> —oswald chambers

8 Why do you think Nehemiah pointed out that only the leaders gathered on the second day to hear God's Law?

9 What did they discover from listening to the Law that day?

10 How did they respond to this new command?

11 As a result of obeying God's Word, the Israelites experienced great joy. How do you show that kind of joy after you've obeyed God's Word?

CONSIDER THE MESSAGE

In chapter 8 of Nehemiah, we come upon one of the most famous revivals in history: the Water Gate Revival. It's a chapter that contains many important lessons for us today as we dwell in a land desperately in need of revival.

To the burning question "What's wrong with America?" the evangelical church has offered some fascinating answers. It's the Hollywood elite. Or the media who are promoting moral decay. No, wait! It's the homosexuals with their activist agenda. Or the liberals in Congress. It's those judges who won't let us pray in public schools. Or the abortion providers.

All convenient scapegoats. But *all wrong*. No, my friends, what America needs is revival. And revival has nothing to do with lost sinners. Dead people can't be revived; only dying people can. Revival is for believers. The Bible could not possibly state this any more plainly, yet somehow the church manages to miss it: "When I shut up the heavens so that there is no rain, or command locusts to devour the land or send a plague among my people, if my people, who are called by my name, will humble themselves and pray and seek my face and turn from their wicked ways, then will I hear from heaven and will forgive their sin and will heal their land. Now my eyes will be open and my ears attentive to the prayers offered in this place" (2 Chronicles 7:13–15).

The Water Gate Revival began when the Israelites gathered "as one man" (v. 1). No Baptists versus Catholics. No charismatics versus fundamentalists. No rich versus poor. There was unity among the believers. Until we are willing to come together, revival will not come to our land.

The Water Gate Revival took shape as the Israelites focused on God's Word, which was honored. (Notice they stood up while it was read.) The people were willing to *listen* and willing to be taught. They weren't critiquing the service. They weren't looking at their watches after forty-five minutes, but they stood attentively from daybreak until noon. And the teachers made sure people understood exactly what God's Word meant.

The people's first response as revival began to break forth in their midst was weeping. Although weeping is a necessary starting point for revival, it can't remain there. Yes, we weep for our sin and the sins of our forefathers. But, thanks to God's grace and mercy, our tears should quickly turn to shouts of joy. A faith comprised solely of tears and guilt trips is misguided; true faith is characterized by celebration. Some people wrongly equate holiness with gloominess. Not so. In Nehemiah, we see holiness sometimes means throwing a party!

However, I believe the most significant criteria for revival had already been fulfilled in Nehemiah 5 and 6. First, the Israelites turned their attention to meeting the needs of the poor. Isaiah 58:5–9 makes it plain that this is a priority for God:

> *Is this the kind of fast I have chosen,*
> *only a day for a man to humble himself?*
> *Is it only for bowing one's head like a reed*
> *and for lying on sackcloth and ashes?*
> *Is that what you call a fast,*
> *a day acceptable to the Lord?*
> *Is not this the kind of fasting I have chosen:*
> *to loose the chains of injustice*
> *and untie the cords of the yoke,*
> *to set the oppressed free*
> *and break every yoke?*
> *Is it not to share your food with the hungry*
> *and to provide the poor wanderer with shelter—*
> *when you see the naked, to clothe him,*
> *and not to turn away from your own flesh and blood?*
> *Then your light will break forth like the dawn,*
> *and your healing will quickly appear;*
> *then your righteousness will go before you,*
> *and the glory of the Lord will be your rear guard.*
> *Then you will call, and the Lord will answer;*
> *you will cry for help, and he will say: Here am I.*

Jesus didn't say, "I was hungry and you prayed God would send me food." Or "I was naked and you fasted for me." He said, "You fed me. You clothed me. You saw my predicament and you actually *did* something about it."

In Nehemiah 6, we noted that the Israelites *completed* the work. They were obedient. Even in the face of threats and intimidation, they kept their hands to the task. Prayer and fasting are no substitute for obedience. We have to do what God tells us to do, how and when he tells us to do it. Then—and only then— will God send revival in our lives and our land.

> Every doctrine that makes *man* the center of God's attention rather than *God* the center of man's devotion hinders Revival.... Revival can come to America—but it will only start when we reject the "me" centered gospel preached so prevalently and realize that the call of God is to serve rather than to be served, to give rather than to get, to lay down our lives rather than to save them. It will come when we begin to pour our hearts out to God in earnest, desiring only His will rather than our will disguised as some "blessing" from above!
>
> –jonathan duttweiler

APPLY THE TRUTH

1 According to this passage, a key to being a joyful believer is obedience to God's Word. How obedient have you been in the past few weeks?

2 Write an action plan for obeying God this week. Remember, obedience starts with hearing (or reading) God's Word and understanding it.

> Obedience is the means whereby we show the earnestness of our desire to do God's will.
>
> –oswald chambers

3 Memorize Nehemiah 8:10:

> **Do not grieve, for the joy of the Lord is your strength.**

Session Nine
Nehemiah 9

Rebuilding Inspires Confession and Repentance

SEARCH THE WORD

1 Using this acrostic, define or describe confession of sin with words or short phrases that begin with these letters:

C

O

N

F

E

S

S

Confession of sins usually doesn't come easily for us. By nature, we tend to be proud and self-sufficient, two characteristics that war against confession. But notice the role of confession in the lives of the Israelites as you study Nehemiah 9.

Read verses 1–3.

2 What effect did God's Word have on the Israelites?

Why?

3 When has God's Word had a similar effect on you?

> The man who can get believers to praying would, under God, usher in the greatest revival that the world has ever known.
> —Leonard ravenhiLL

Read verses 4-15.

4 How did the Levites direct the people's attention to God?

5 For what did they praise God?

6 What was God's relationship with Abraham?

7 What did God do for the Israelites?

8 What do you learn about God from these summaries of history?

Read verses 16-31.

9 How did the people respond to God's loving actions (vv. 16–18)?

Why?

10 In contrast, how did God act toward them (vv. 19–25)?

11 What is the most surprising aspect of God's love that's recounted here?

12 Verses 26–31 summarize the book of Judges. What sinful pattern did the Israelites go through with God?

Read verses 32–38.

13 As this long prayer ends, what did the Levites acknowledge about God?

> Poverty-stricken as the Church is today in many things, she is most stricken here, in the place of prayer. We have many organizers, but few agonizers; many players and payers, but few pray-ers; many singers, few clingers; lots of pastors, few wrestlers; many fears, few tears; much fashion, little passion; many interferers, few intercessors; many writers, but few fighters. Failing here, we fail everywhere.
> —Leonard ravenhiLL

About their people?

About themselves?

14 What did they do as a result of this knowledge and their current situation?

CONSIDER THE MESSAGE

Confession and repentance. Could there be two less popular topics in the world today? Yet they have been set before us in Nehemiah 9 as the Israelites come to grips with their sin. More to the point, they finally admit that their circumstances are the logical out-come of their own choices (and the choices of their forefathers).

If you want to make people angry, try this: Tell them they are where they are because of the choices they have made. Oh my! Peo-ple do *not* want to hear that. Trust me, I know from personal expe-rience. It's his parent's fault. It's her husband's fault. It's his ex-wife's fault. It's his boss's fault. Or her plight is the result of some fluke or the consequence of living in an unjust universe. You might even hear my all-time pet peeve excuse: I guess God has just *allowed* this. It's the old "I've been living on coffee and doughnuts for thirty years and haven't walked farther than the mailbox in the past decade—but I guess God *allowed* me to contract diabetes."

I want to s-c-r-e-a-m! Confess! Repent! Take responsibility for your sin and its consequences!

In your study of the text, you no doubt noted that the prayer included a point-by-point recitation of Israel's sins. Charles Finney, widely regarded as the greatest revival preacher in church history, led more than half a million people to Christ in the early 1800s. More significantly, his converts were actually converted. Today, when a great evangelistic campaign sweeps through a city, not only is the city unchanged, the church is largely unchanged. Not so with Finney. Entire communities were turned upside down by his preaching. It was not uncommon for bar gatherings to be trans-formed into prayer meetings and for courthouses to be left with no cases to put on trial.

Finney left behind a great volume of writings, all expounding on his firm conviction that whenever the people of God earnestly con-fess and repent of their sins, turning to him in "agonizing prayer" as he termed it, God will send revival. Finney explained exactly what he meant by confession and repentance:

> *Look back over your past history. Take up your individ-ual sins one by one, and look at them. I do not mean that you should just cast a glance at your past life, and see that it has been full of sins, and then go to God and make a sort of general confession, and ask for pardon. That is not the way.*

You must take them up one by one. It will be a good thing to take a pen and paper, as you go over them, and write them down as they occur to you. Go over them as carefully as a merchant goes over his books; and as often as a sin comes before your memory, add it to the list. General confessions of sin will never do. Your sins were committed one by one; and as far as you can come at them, they ought to be reviewed and repented of one by one.[1]

Finney then went on to list common sins, the first of which is ingratitude. Is that not the ultimate American sin? We are the richest nation in the history of the world. Yet, rather than being grateful for God's provisions, we are discontented and constantly clamoring for more. Then Finney mentioned neglecting the Bible, prayer, and such other "means of grace" as public worship; lack of compassion in general and unconcern for the lost, specifically; and last but not least, selfishness and a complete disregard for Christ's command and example of self-denial. These are the sins of omission. Finney then turned his attention to the sins of commission: pride, envy, slander (gossip), lying, cheating, robbing God by withholding your tithe, squandering your time in vain pursuits, and temper. I was amazed that Finney didn't even *mention* the sins we consider the "biggies"; instead, he focused on nice, polite, church sins. In other words, the sins of the heart.

I urge you, even as I urge myself, to prayerfully reread the extensive prayer in this chapter of Nehemiah. Ask God to reveal to you in what ways you have behaved as the Israelites. Next, pray through Finney's list of common sins. Take his advice. Get out a pen and paper. Write down, one by one, every sin you can recall. Yes, every sin. Then lay it at the foot of the cross.

Even as we saw the Israelites weep in Nehemiah 8, you may weep as you survey your list. But God's objective is not to make you cry: "For you became sorrowful as God intended and so were not harmed in any way by us. Godly sorrow brings repentance that leads to salvation and leaves no regret, but worldly sorrow brings death. See what this godly sorrow has produced in you: what earnestness, what eagerness to clear yourselves, what indignation, what alarm, what longing, what concern, what readiness to see justice done" (2 Corinthians 7:9–11).

God wants to lead you to repentance. You may begin with tears, but you, too, will discover great joy. "Those who sow in tears will reap with songs of joy. He who goes out weeping, carrying seed to sow, will return with songs of joy, carrying sheaves with him" (Psalm 126:5–6).

Nehemiah 9 ends with the Israelites making a binding agreement and *putting it in writing*. Why not do the same? Why not write out your agreement with the Lord, agreeing with Him about your past sins and pledging yourself to go and sin no more?

APPLY THE TRUTH

1 Notice the pattern in the prayer in this chapter: praise, rehearsal of God's works, confession of sins, repentance (change of behavior, indicated by the binding agreement with God to obey Him). Spend some time in prayer, following this same pattern.

2 Write out your agreement with God, agreeing with Him about your past sins and pledging to go and sin no more.

From the day of Pentecost, there has been *not one* great spiritual awakening in any land which has not begun in a *union of prayer*, though only among two or three; no such outward, upward movement has continued after such prayer meetings declined.

–a. t. pierson

3 Memorize Nehemiah 9:38:

In view of all this, we are making a binding agreement, putting it in writing, and our leaders, our Levites and our priests are affixing their seals to it.

Session Ten
Nehemiah 10

Rebuilding Calls for Renewed Dedication

SEARCH THE WORD

1 What kinds of contracts have you signed?

What motivated you to sign them?

If you're like most adults, you've signed at least a couple of contracts: mortgage papers, car loan, apartment lease, business partnership, standards of behavior while in college or working for a Christian organization, marriage license, etc. But have you ever signed a covenant, or contract, with God? Hmm. It's something to think about as you study Nehemiah 10.

Read verses 1-27.

2 After listening to the Law read and explained, then obeying it, the Israelites signed a written covenant with God. Why do you think Nehemiah included this list of people who signed it?

3 What was the point of signing a covenant instead of verbally expressing their renewed dedication to God?

"Mind your own business" is not a Christian phrase. We are called and commanded to be involved in each other's lives.
–rick warren

Read verses 28-31.

4 What do the categories of people who joined the leaders in making this covenant tell you?

5 What did they commit to do?

6 Why was it important that they agreed not to intermarry?

7 How serious was this commitment?

> **By rehearsing the terms of the covenant and promising to observe the law, the people were committing themselves to making the things of God a sacred priority.**
> –j. karl Laney

Read verses 32–39.

8 What practical obligations were they taking on?

9 What provisions did they make for the priests and the temple?

10 How did they intend to handle the collection of goods mentioned in this covenant?

11 How do you think these actions with material goods affected their spiritual lives?

12 If you were to write a covenant like this for your church or small group, what would you include?

CONSIDER THE MESSAGE

There's safety in numbers and power in accountability. It wasn't enough for the Israelites to pray their vow silently before the Lord. It wasn't even enough for them to make "a binding agreement, putting it in writing," which is where we left off in the last chapter. No, if they were to have any chance of making a national about-face, one further step was required: accountability. It's precisely what is lacking in churches today.

I attend a megachurch. Quite frankly, I think it's the greatest church on the planet. And you have no idea who is saying this: the former Queen of Church Critiquing. But as much as I love it, I also see an inherent danger: It's easy for people to be lulled into complacency. They can tell themselves, "Hey, I attend a dynamic church; *and,* as an added bonus, no one asks me difficult questions, like 'Why haven't you been here for the last three weeks?' But no problem. I have enough sense to go to a great church when I *do* attend, so I must be doing fine." Our pastor readily admits that we have a different congregation every Sunday, as the average regular attendee turns up only twice a month.

There's simply no accountability unless you actively seek it. The proliferation of megachurches explains, to some extent, the modern phenomenon wherein millions of Americans claim to be "born-again" Christians yet America becomes increasingly decadent with each passing day. What's worse, the average Christian is literally indistinguishable from his or her non-Christian neighbor or co-worker.

In contrast, Nehemiah compiled a list of everyone who agreed to the binding covenant. Then he published it for all the world to see, for generations to come. That's accountability! Anyone with access to that list could turn to anyone on the list, any day of the week, and say, "Wait a minute! You're working on Saturday? You signed that covenant pledging yourself not to do business on the Sabbath. What's up with that?" Whoa.

What are you willing to put your name to—and publish for all the world to see? Would you be willing to put up a Web page, listing all the sins you plan to abstain from and inviting the planet to hold you accountable? It might look something like this: "I hereby vow, before the Lord and the whole world, never to gossip or complain again. Anyone overhearing me gossiping or complaining can take me to task. Further, you can report the date and time right here on this Web page. Simply complete the form at the bottom of this page."

I can recommend an excellent Web site creation software program if you like. What? Not interested?

Accountability! Who asks you the tough questions? Who knows your pet sins? Who looks you in the eye and courageously confronts you with the truth of your life? Have you given anyone both the opportunity and the permission to get that close? You should—for your own sake.

This chapter includes some extraordinary statements and commitments. Among other things, it says some of the people "separated themselves from the neighboring peoples for the sake of the Law of God" (v. 28). Now, that is *not* politically correct at all, is it? But let me ask you: Is there someone—or a group of someones—you need to separate yourself from, not *only* for your sake but for the sake of the Law of God? In other words, spending time with those people literally leads you to sin.

A basic tenet of Alcoholics Anonymous is that you don't spend time with active alcoholics. In fact, you don't even hang out with your favorite former drinking buddies who've found their way to sobriety. Too risky! I'm not saying you need to be elitist or judgmental. Not saying you should declare yourself "too good" for certain people. I am saying: Be honest with yourself *and* with someone who's willing to hold you accountable.

The Israelites pledged themselves "to obey carefully all the commands, regulations and decrees of the Lord our Lord" (v. 29). All of them? Not just the commands they like? Obedience is another unpopular term in our day. But it's the secret to spiritual power, not to mention a requirement of our Holy God.

"We promise," the Israelites said in writing. If promises meant *anything* in today's society, zillions of lawyers would be out of business by morning. But alas, promises are empty. Our promise extends only to the point where fulfilling our word becomes inconvenient. But the Bible says we should keep our oath even when it hurts. Or, as the Amplified Bible renders it, "swear to your own hurt" (Psalm 15:4).

The Israelites weren't messing around. Instead, they further pledged, "We assume the responsibility for carrying out the commands" to give to God's house and provide for its maintenance (v. 32). Assume responsibility? Oh my, my, my! No one assumes responsibility anymore. It's everyone else's job, not ours. (Hey, it's not my department!) Besides, we're too busy placing blame instead. They gave God their *firstfruits* before they were sure the *second* fruits would come in. Most of us give God our leftovers, if anything.

Last but not least, in their binding agreement they declared, "We will not neglect the house of our God" (v. 39). You *are* the house of God. You *are* the temple of the Holy Spirit. When's the last time the temple had a thorough cleansing? I don't mean in the shower! I mean spiritual cleansing. A promise not to neglect God's house is a promise to keep your soul and spirit clean, as 1 John 1:9 reminds us: "If we confess our sins, he is faithful and just to forgive us our sins and to cleanse us from all unrighteousness" (ESV).

So we've come full circle. Renewed dedication comes back to confession and repentance. And that just makes sense, doesn't it? The purpose and outcome of accountability is cleansed, purified lives that glorify God. That's why we're on the planet. We might as well acknowledge that truth—and put it in writing.

APPLY THE TRUTH

Israel's overall commitment
was thus something very
much to admire. It was an
expression of radical
repentance, which meant a
change of mind, heart, and
life; a gesture of full
consecration, which meant
being separated from other
people of God; and a gateway
into the life of faith, in
which God would be relied
on for everything.

–j. i. packer

1 What areas of your life do you need to commit or rededicate to God?

2 If you're serious about this dedication, write a covenant with God, detailing specific actions and including an accountability provision to help you keep it.

3 Memorize Nehemiah 10:39:

We will not neglect the house of our God.

Session Eleven
Nehemiah 11–12

Rebuilding Requires an Army of Servants

SEARCH THE WORD

1 How often do you volunteer for or just do behind-the-scenes jobs that no one else knows you do and for which you get little or no credit?

How does such volunteering affect you?

Most people prefer the jobs that get the glory or at least the thanks. But no matter what jobs we choose to do, we can't do them all. For example, it takes an army of servants to accomplish God's work, as Nehemiah 11 and 12 demonstrate.

Read 11:1-36.

2 Why did a tenth of the people move to Jerusalem? (See 7:4.)

3 Why do you think many people didn't want to live in Jerusalem?

> **In all ages, men have preferred their own ease and advantage to the public good.**
> -matthew henry

4 How do you think these people felt to have Nehemiah leave a record of their names?

Read 12:1-26.

5 Why do you think Nehemiah mentioned all these priests and Levites by name?

6 Why do you think Nehemiah singled out Mattaniah to include his job description (v. 8)?

Read 12:27-43.

7 Why were the Levites brought to Jerusalem?

8 If you had been part of that crowd, how would you have described the celebration to someone who wasn't there?

It is good to know what our godly predecessors were, that we may learn what we should be.
–matthew henry

9 How would you have felt?

10 How did the Israelites feel?

Why?

11 What effect would their rejoicing have had on the people around them?

Read 12:44-47.

12 How did the people take care of the physical needs of the priests and Levites?

Why?

13 Usually it's the up-front people who get recognition, but Nehemiah singled out some of those in supporting roles, including the storeroom people and gatekeepers. In what ways does recognizing others contribute to joyful worship?

CONSIDER THE MESSAGE

Okay, admit it. I know what you just did. And the reason I know is because I did the same thing, even though I am sitting here writing a book about Nehemiah.

What am I talking about? Skimming. That's what we do when we come to a list of unpronounceable names in the Bible. We skim through. Of course, that's an improvement. In the days before *The Prayer of Jabez,* most of us didn't even skim. We flat-out skipped. But we've learned our lesson. Now we skim to see if any of those names has a little added commentary that might translate into a *New York Times* bestseller–worthy degree of insight.

Back when I wasn't nearly as sanctified as I am now, I used to watch the old TV show *Cheers.* It's the sort of show Christians shouldn't waste time watching, but alas, I admit doing it anyway. Since God can bring something good out of anything, He redeemed my useless television time by imparting to my heart a vitally important life lesson. It comes from the opening song about wanting to go where everybody knows our name. We all want to feel like we matter. That if we show up, people will be glad. And if we don't show up, someone will notice our absence.

Once upon a time, I overheard several church leaders discussing a dilemma: The woman who cleaned the communion cups had moved away, and no one had stepped in to replace her—and communion Sunday was only days away. Until that moment, it had never occurred to me that *someone* washed the communion cups. Then I read a story about women gathering together to bake communion bread. Hadn't thought of that either. There are churches all over the world that enjoy freshly baked bread for communion, and *someone* bakes it. Our church uses tiny crackers, and I'm sure *someone* has to order them, store them, divide them up, and put them onto the plates for 4,500 people. *Someone* has to fill 4,500 little communion cups once a month.

Ever think of that? Me neither.

I recently arrived at my church for a Monday morning prayer meeting only to discover that the prayer room looked like a war zone. And, well, I guess that's exactly what it *is* after all. The teens had met in there Sunday night. Apparently God showed up, too, because there were tear-soaked tissues strewn all over the floor. Folding chairs were placed haphazardly around the room in various formations where twos and threes had gathered together in His name. Snack crumbs crunched under my heels as I walked around surveying the remnants of a hard-fought battle. You may think less of me for saying this, but here goes: Before it occurred to me that the room had been used precisely as God intended, the thought drifted through my mind, *Why didn't* someone *clean this place up?*

Then a voice inside me made a radical suggestion: *You* are someone, aren't you?

Scenes like these occur day after day, week after week at churches around the world. Countless thousands, maybe even *millions* of people labor silently, in the background, so the work of Christ can continue through His church. Nobody knows their names. They don't draw attention to themselves. They don't have flashy ministries. They serve in obscurity.

Think about your church for a moment. *Someone* types, prints, and folds the bulletins. *Someone* turns the lights on and off and controls the all-important thermostat. *Someone* cleans the rest rooms, vacuums the carpets, mops the floors. *Someone.* Do you know who?

We may skip through the long list of names, not only in Nehemiah 11 and 12, but Nehemiah 7 and 10 as well. We may wonder why God "wasted" so much valuable space in the Bible. I mean, why not cut the names and insert something we can all enjoy, like a nice psalm or even a moving prayer like the one we read in chapter 9? I'd like to suggest two reasons why God gave "press" to people whose names we will quickly forget, if we bother to read them at all.

There are more than 750 "Halls of Fame" in America and more than 450 "Who's Who" publications, but you won't find many real servants in these places. Notoriety means nothing to real servants because they know the difference between prominence and significance.... The most significant service is often the service that is unseen.

—rick warren

First, God allowed biblical authors to express their individuality through their writings, even as they were led by the Holy Spirit. We gain valuable insight into Nehemiah's character by pondering these lists. *He gave credit where it was due.* He wasn't pretending to be a one-man show who single-handedly rebuilt the city walls and reestablished worship in Jerusalem. By including these names, Nehemiah was saying to the world, "Rebuilding required an army of servants, and let me tell you who they were." Some leaders think they are above the janitor, the nursery workers, and communion-cup cleaners. Not Nehemiah. *He knew their names.* He knew their contributions deserved recognition.

Second, I believe the Holy Spirit allowed Nehemiah to include these lists as a reminder to God's people throughout the centuries: It takes an army of servants to accomplish God's work on earth. And you can't all be in the limelight. You can't all be the center of attention. Sometimes you serve in seeming obscurity. But God sees you, and He has written *your* name down in his book. One day, "your Father, who sees what is done in secret, will reward you" (Matthew 6:4). The Amplified Bible takes it a step further, saying God "will reward you openly."

So stay faithful. Serve your local church any way you can—even if no one knows your name. Remember, God does. And that service will bring you great joy.

APPLY THE TRUTH

1 Think about your local church. What jobs can you do regularly for a year or in the next couple of weeks to help accomplish God's work in and through your congregation?

2 If you have difficulty serving in obscurity, ask God to change your attitude. Also spend time praising and thanking God for His working in your life and the joy you've received as a result.

3 Memorize Nehemiah 12:43:

> **And on that day they offered great sacri-
> fices, rejoicing because God had given them
> great joy. The women and children also
> rejoiced. The sound of rejoicing in Jerusalem
> could be heard far away.**

Session Twelve
Nehemiah 13

Rebuilding Requires Periodic Renewal

SEARCH THE WORD

1 When have you failed to keep a promise you made to God?

What did you do to make it right?

Read verses 1-3.

Between chapters 12 and 13, Nehemiah returned to Babylon for an unknown period of time (v. 6, perhaps as long as two years) after completing his first term as governor of Judah. When he came back to Jerusalem for his second term, he discovered the people had strayed from the covenant they had signed. To get them back on track with God, God's Word was read to the people again.

2 How did the people respond to what they heard from God's Word?

Read verses 4–14.

3 What sin had Eliashib committed?

> Where God has sent reformation, Satan will work, behind the scenes if not overtly, for deformation of all that was made new.
>
> –j. i. packer

Why was this wrong?

4 What did Nehemiah do when he found out?

5 When Nehemiah discovered the Levites, priests, and singers had gone back to their farms, what did he do about this situation?

6 What did Nehemiah pray in relation to the temple reforms?

Read verses 15-22.

7 How were the people living on the Sabbath?

8 Why was it important to keep the Sabbath holy?

9 What actions did Nehemiah take to encourage the people to keep the Sabbath for God and not themselves?

10 What did Nehemiah pray in relation to this reform?

Read verses 23-29.

11 Why did Nehemiah react so harshly to those who had sinned by marrying foreigners?

12 How did Nehemiah's prayer differ from his previous ones recorded in this chapter?

Read verses 30-31.

13 As Nehemiah concluded his memoirs, what accomplishments were most important to him?

> **He will be remembered by all, not only as a gifted administrator, but also as a devoted servant of God whose life exemplifies that delicate balance between faithfulness in prayer and diligence in work.**
>
> –j. carL Laney

14 Why do you think he mentioned these?

15 Why do you think his last prayer request was for God's favor?

CONSIDER THE MESSAGE

Something new. That's what we all clamor for: new clothes, new cars, even a new "word" from God. However, the Christian life is not so much about new as it is about renew. Once we've heard the truth, the challenge is living according to it. The daily walk of faith is not always exciting, as the people of Nehemiah's day discovered. After their glorious Water Gate Revival—when they discovered the

Word of God and made new vows and covenants—they settled in for the hard task of living out their commitments.

And that's precisely where most of us get into trouble. We have no problems on the mountaintop. No trouble when it's all new and exciting. It's the day after day, day after day, daily-ness that trips us up. Our initial enthusiasm wanes. We drift away. And usually the drifting occurs so gradually that we don't even notice.

That's where godly leaders like Nehemiah come in. They sound the alarm. They rebuke us, standing in our midst saying, "WAKE UP! Look how far you've fallen. Return to God. Return to God's Word and return to the service of the Lord." It is the role of spiritual leaders or friends to call us back to our commitments, challenging us to experience renewal. It's so important to have people in your life who have the courage to rebuke you, people who love you enough to challenge you. Nehemiah wasn't playing church with these people. He got right in their faces, forcefully confronting them with their sin. In fact, he admitted, "I beat some of the men and pulled out their hair" (v. 25). And I think my pastor's tough on me because he preaches convicting sermons!

I used to worry that it was unbiblical for me to routinely threaten my audiences by saying, "Y'all better get it together, or I'll come smack you upside your heads!" Now I realize what terrific company I'm in! Over the years, I've often challenged people with these words: "Do you have a Nathan in your life?" Nathan was the prophet who confronted David concerning his adulterous affair with Bathsheba (2 Samuel 12). Afterward, David penned these words: "Create in me a pure heart, O God, and renew a steadfast spirit within me. Do not cast me from your presence or take your Holy Spirit from me. Restore to me the joy of your salvation and grant me a willing spirit, to sustain me" (Psalm 51:10–12).

A "Nathan" is someone who loves you enough to confront your sin and who does so in such a way that you are led to repentance and renewal. Well, apparently a "Nehemiah" serves the same purpose. He reminded the Israelites that they had done the *very thing* they vowed not to do. They had made a solemn oath: "We will not neglect the house of our God" (10:39). Yet we can clearly see, through Nehemiah's vivid portrayal, that that's exactly what they had done. God's house had been completely neglected.

You can call it backsliding or a besetting sin, but isn't that exactly what we do? We return to the same sin we repented of most passionately. We do the same thing we vowed *not* to do and neglect those things we promised *to* do. People are the same yesterday, today, and forever—until Jesus takes us home to glory.

Is it time for renewal in your life? Although this definition isn't found in *Vine's Expository Dictionary* or Webster's dictionary, I'll share it because I think it's helpful. I once heard a preacher give a beautiful picture of repentance. We've all heard of the penthouse, right? It's the highest place in the building, the top floor apartment or condominium. Well, re-pent-ance is returning to your highest place with the Lord.

Can you recall the highest place you ever experienced in your relationship with the Lord? Maybe it was the week you spent at summer camp in high school. Or a women's retreat you once attended. Can you honestly say that, right now, you are at the highest place with the Lord? You've never been closer to Him? Never been more passionate about your faith? Never more eager to fulfill your vows and serve God wholeheartedly?

If not, why not? Do you need to confess and repent of sin in your life? How can you return to that highest place? Do you simply need a time of refreshing and renewal?

Nehemiah knew it was time for renewal because the house of God was a wreck. There was no worship. People were not bringing their offerings. And the temple was filled with junk that had no place being there. "Do you not know that your body is a temple of the Holy Spirit, who is in you, whom you have received from God?" (1 Corinthians 6:19). Dear temple, are *you* filled with worship? Or do you feel like your internal worship leader has left the building? Do you feel like you have nothing left to offer God? Maybe there are things in your temple that simply do not belong there, and it's time to toss that stuff out.

The storerooms of your temple are your spirit, soul, and body. The Bible commands us, "Since we have these promises, dear friends, let us purify ourselves from everything that contaminates body and spirit, perfecting holiness out of reverence for God"

(2 Corinthians 7:1). Maybe you need to purify your temple—purify your spirit, soul, and body. We see in this chapter that the priestly office had been defiled. As believers in Christ, we are the priests. Are we defiling the priestly office? One of the major mistakes the Israelites made was putting the wrong person in charge of the temple. Don't make the same mistake. Don't let other people tell you who or what you should let into your life. "Oh, this movie isn't so bad." Or "Joan means well; she just has a problem with gossip."

Take the command to purify your life seriously. Then, and only then, can you pray as Nehemiah did, "Remember me with favor, O my God" (v. 31b).

I can honestly say that, at this moment, I am at one of my highest places with the Lord. Writing this book has been one of the most joyous experiences of my life. In fact, I've been almost giddy as I've studied and prayed about revival and renewal. I believe the reason I am at such a high place is the same reason the Israelites were able to experience renewal. The secret is found in Nehemiah 13:1: God's Word was being read aloud in their midst.

For the past few weeks, I've been reading God's Word aloud every day as part of the 90-Day Renewal program I am leading at my local church. Women who've already completed the renewal have experienced absolutely miraculous results. One woman led her seventy-year-old husband to Christ on day sixty-three of her journey; others have been healed physically and emotionally. This is my fourth trip through the content, and even though I wrote it, my life is being completely renewed because the book consists primarily of God's Word, organized into daily Bible readings, Scripture prayers, and Scripture-based affirmations.

If you are wondering what to do now that you've come to the end of this study on the book of Nehemiah, I urge you to prayerfully consider undertaking the 90-Day Renewal, based on my book *Becoming the Woman I Want to Be: A 90-Day Journey to Renewing Spirit, Soul, and Body.* For information, visit my Web site at *www.donnapartow.com.* Get ready to purify yourself of everything that contaminates spirit, soul, and body. And get ready for renewal.

I leave you with a Scripture prayer:

Therefore, my dear friends, do not lose heart. Though outwardly we are wasting away, yet inwardly we are being renewed day by day. For our light and momentary troubles are achieving for us an eternal glory that far outweighs them all. So let us fix our eyes not on what is seen, but on what is unseen. For what is seen is temporary, but what is unseen is eternal (2 Corinthians 4:16–18, author's paraphrase).

Lord God, we ask you to renew us in spirit, soul, and body. Lead us to the highest place in our relationship with you that our lives may be effective and productive for your Kingdom. Amen

APPLY THE TRUTH

> **Revival is a series of new beginnings.**
> –david mckee

1 Ask God to show you any sin in your life that you need to deal with; then confess it to Him and ask for His forgiveness.

2 What steps can you take this week to keep from slipping back into the same sins?

3 Memorize Nehemiah 13:22b and 31b:

> **Remember me for this also, O my God, and show mercy to me according to your great love. . . . Remember me with favor, O my God.**

Leader's Guide

TO ENCOURAGE GROUP DISCUSSION

- If your group isn't used to discussing together, explain at the beginning of the first session that these studies are designed for discussion, not lecture. Encourage each member to participate, but keep in mind that it may take several meetings before shy members feel comfortable enough to participate.
- Encourage discussion by asking several people to contribute answers to a question. "What do the rest of you think?" or "Is there anything else that could be added?" are two ways of doing this.
- Receive all contributions warmly. Never bluntly reject what anyone says, even if you think the answer is incorrect. Instead, ask what others think and/or ask the person to identify the verse(s) that led her to that conclusion.
- Be sure you don't talk too much as the leader. Redirect questions that you are asked. A discussion should move in the form of a bouncing ball, back and forth between members, not in the form of a fan with the discussion always coming back to the leader at that point. The leader acts as a moderator. As members of a group get to know one another better, the discussion will move more freely.
- Don't be afraid of pauses or long silences. People need time to think about the questions. Never answer your own question—either rephrase it or move on to another area for discussion.
- Watch hesitant members for an indication by facial expression or body language that they have something to say, and then give them an encouraging nod or speak their names.
- Discourage too-talkative members from monopolizing the discussion by specifically directing questions to others. If necessary,

speak to them privately about the need for discussion and enlist their help in encouraging everyone to participate.

- End the sessions by praying for one another, thanking God for growth and asking Him for help to practice the truth discovered during the week. Vary the prayer times by staying together, breaking into smaller groups or pairs, using sentence prayers, etc. Resist the ever-present temptation to spend more time talking about prayer than actually praying. When it's time to pray, don't waste time on elaborate prayer requests for Susie's uncle's cousin's neighbor's grandmother. Instead, allow the Holy Spirit to bring forth what is on His heart as He prompts individual members to pray.

DISCUSSION LEADER'S NOTES

1: Rebuilding Is Rooted in Prayer: Nehemiah 1

Purpose: To understand the necessity of prayer and to follow Nehemiah's example in this area.

Question 1: Each study begins with an icebreaker question, such as this one. Ask a few volunteers to share their answers. As your group members get to know one another better, you may want to go around the circle and have everyone respond to this opening question. Pray for sensitivity in how you use it so you don't embarrass anyone or put people on the spot.

Question 2: The Babylonians destroyed Jerusalem's walls and gates 140 years earlier, leaving the people who still lived there vulnerable to attacks. Although the Israelites had begun to rebuild the walls thirteen years earlier, they did not complete the task.

Question 5: Nehemiah's reaction was typical of how Jewish people responded to tragedy. See Ezra 9:3–5.

Question 11: As cupbearer to the king, Nehemiah had an important and influential job. In addition to tasting wine before it was given to the king to be sure it wasn't poisoned, he was also in charge of the finances. Thus he had direct access to the king, which was not afforded to everyone.

Conclusion: Sing together "I Will Call Upon the Lord" or "Unto Thee, O Lord." (Several studies conclude with a song to sing together. If your group doesn't know the suggested song(s), choose another one on the same theme.)

2: Rebuilding Takes Preparation: Nehemiah 2

Purpose: To understand the value of adequate preparation and planning before beginning a job or project.

Question 2: The month of Nisan corresponds to our March/April. The year was 444 B.C.

Question 3: For Nehemiah to let the king see his sadness was risky. He could have been fired or killed since the king could have interpreted sadness as dissatisfaction with the king.

Question 10: Be sure your group members understand that God doesn't "bless" us in ways that are contrary to His Word. If anyone mentions something that is clearly unbiblical, take a minute to clarify God's position, but do not spend a lot of time on the issue. You may need to say, "Let's talk about that after we finish the study."

Question 15: Sanballat was governor of Samaria. Previously, he had had oversight of Jerusalem and Judah, which accounts for his opposition against Nehemiah. Tobiah was a foreigner.

Conclusion: Pray for group members who are in the preparation/planning stage of a project. Ask volunteers to read Proverbs 16:3–4; 16:9; and 19:21.

3: Rebuilding Requires Teamwork: Nehemiah 3

Purpose: To recognize the value of teamwork in doing God's work.

Question 2: It was common in Nehemiah's day for the leader to assign sections to specific groups of people to do work like this.

Question 3: The word *dedicated* in verse 1 means "set apart." It probably involved a groundbreaking ceremony.

Question 9: The casual way Nehemiah mentioned women working with men indicates it was a common occurrence.

Conclusion: Close by reading together Ephesians 4:11–15.

4: Nehemiah 4: Rebuilding Invites Opposition

Purpose: To recognize that following God is often accompanied by opposition, which we can meet with prayer and work.

Question 4: Nehemiah's prayer is similar to some of the psalms, such as 7; 35; 58; 59; 83; 109; and 137, in which the authors asked God to condemn or judge their enemies. Nehemiah prayed for the application of the Abrahamic covenant—that God would curse those who cursed or threatened the Jewish people (Genesis 12:3). "Do not cover up their guilt" (v. 5) is a request for punishment for their sins. Keep in mind that Nehemiah was not asking for personal vengeance.

Question 5: Notice that Nehemiah didn't wait around for something to happen after he prayed. Instead, he went to work, doing what he could.

Question 9: If you have time, ask for a couple of brief testimonies of how focusing on God in the midst of opposition and trials helped people get through them.

Conclusion: Close by reading 1 Corinthians 15:58 together.

5: Nehemiah 5: Rebuilding Develops Compassion for Others

Purpose: To show compassion to people instead of taking advantage of them.

Question 2: It was common for people to sell their children as slaves in order to keep their land and pay their debts; they hoped to redeem their children later when they could afford to.

Question 5: The Law prohibited Israelites from charging usury, or interest, on a loan. See Exodus 22:25 and Leviticus 25:36–37. Loans were acts of charity, not ways to make money.

Question 6: Based on his character, we can conclude that Nehemiah was not charging interest for the loans he made to needy individuals. He practiced what he preached.

The "hundredth part of the money" (v. 11) refers to the interest people were charging, one percent per month, or twelve percent per year.

Question 8: Ask a volunteer to read Ecclesiastes 5:4–5.

Conclusion: Play a recording of NewSong's "Light Your World," Bruce Carroll's "Who Will Be Jesus," or Casting Crown's "If We Are the Body."

6: Rebuilding Continues Through Discernment: Nehemiah 6:1-14

Purpose: To ask God for discernment in dealing with people, so we won't be deceived.

Question 2: The plain of Ono was about twenty-seven miles northwest of Jerusalem, more than a day's journey.

Question 5: The fact that Sanballat's letter was unsealed pretty much guaranteed that the contents would become public knowledge. If the rumor of a revolt got back to the Persian king, Nehemiah and his people would be quelled immediately.

Question 9: It was against the Law for anyone other than the priests to enter the sanctuary of the temple (Numbers 3:10; 18:7).

Question 12: Emphasize to your group how much Nehemiah prayed. If you have time, you might want to look at the pattern of his prayers so far.

Conclusion: Close with Paul's prayer in Philippians 1:9–11.

7: Rebuilding Requires Completion: Nehemiah 6:15-7:73a

Purpose: To finish the tasks God gives us to do.

Question 3: The fact that the Israelites' enemies were afraid when the wall was finished means that they were in awe of what the Jewish people and their God accomplished in such a short time.

Question 6: Note that Nehemiah recognized he couldn't do the job by himself, so he recruited assistants. Discuss briefly how this strategy is a sign of good leadership.

Question 9: Note that 7:4–69 is almost the same as Ezra 2:1–64. "These Jews were the 'living link' that connected the historic past with the prophetic future and made it possible for Jesus Christ to come into the world. Ezra 2 and Nehemiah 7 are to the Old Testament what Hebrews 11 is to the New Testament: a listing of the people whose faith and courage made things happen."[1]

Conclusion: Challenge your group members to live so Paul's testimony in 2 Timothy 4:6–7 will be theirs too.

8: Rebuilding Unleashes Revival: Nehemiah 7:73b–8:18

Purpose: To understand that spiritual revival is the result of obeying God's Word.

Question 2: For background on Ezra and his ministry, read Ezra 7–10.

Scribes could read Hebrew; had the skills to copy, transcribe, and compose manuscripts; were widely read in literature; had studied Scripture; and were experts in the Law. Many were also priests.

Standing was a sign of respect (Ezekiel 2:1).

Question 3: Note that it's not enough to know God's Word; we need to understand and practice it too.

Question 5: If you have time, ask a couple of volunteers to tell about a time when they heard or read God's Word, were convicted by it, and obeyed it.

Question 10: See Leviticus 23:33–44 for the institution of the feast of booths, or tabernacles, known today as *Sukkot*. This joyous festival begins five days after the Day of Atonement (*Yom Kippur*) and is a precursor to the American Thanksgiving day. For one week, the Israelites lived in booths as a reminder of their wandering in the wilderness in temporary structures. Plus they rejoiced in the grain harvest that God had provided for them.

Conclusion: Sing together "Shine, Jesus, Shine" or "Trust and Obey."

9: Rebuilding Inspires Confession and Repentance: Nehemiah 9

Purpose: To confess our sins and repent of them in order to live to please God.

Question 3. Watch your time, so you don't let this question eat up too much of it. You may want to ask for only two or three volunteers to answer this question.

Question 8: Reviewing Israel's history in prayers and psalms was common in the Bible (e.g., Psalm 78; 105; 135; 136) but not among other nations. Besides helping people to focus on what God had done for them and how big He is, this retelling helped people who didn't have written copies of Scripture to learn and remember their history as a nation.

Question 11: Try to let a number of group members answer this question. Doing so will highlight aspects others didn't think about.

Question 14: A seal was a symbol of authority and a way to keep a letter private.

Conclusion: Spend a few minutes in silent prayer, asking God to reveal your sin and confessing it to Him. Close by reading Psalm 51 and/or singing together "Cleanse Me" or "Change My Heart, O God."

10: Rebuilding Calls for Renewed Dedication: Nehemiah 10

Purpose: To recognize that accountability is necessary for lasting obedience to God.

Question 5: For the law on keeping the Sabbath, see Exodus 20:8–11. For a fuller explanation of the "seventh year" Sabbath, read Exodus 23:10–11; Leviticus 25:2–7; and Deuteronomy 15:1–3.

Question 6: For background on this commitment, see Deuteronomy 7:1–6 and Ezra 9:1–2.

Conclusion: Ask two volunteers to read James 5:16 and Galatians 6:1–4.

11: Rebuilding Requires an Army of Servants: Nehemiah 11–12

Purpose: To acknowledge that no one can do God's work alone and we're all important in ministry.

Question 3: Although Jerusalem was "the holy city," it was not a desirable place to live in Nehemiah's day. It had not fully recovered from the devastation of war, and it was in an area that Israel's enemies wanted. Besides, most people wouldn't want to abandon their farms and risk losing their land to move to the city.

Question 5: This genealogy of priests and Levites would have been important in establishing the continuity of the priestly line then and in the future.

Question 11: The fact that leaders and choirs walked along the top of the walls showed the Israelites' enemies how strong they were, in contrast to the earlier taunts of those enemies (4:3).

Conclusion: To illustrate the importance of all believers working together to accomplish God's work, read together 1 Corinthians 12. To help group members get a feel for being part of the Body, you might want to ask a member to write out this chapter as a choral reading. Have her label sections of this passage as trunk, legs, and arms. Before this session, outline a body shape on the floor with tape. Have group members stand in the trunk, arms, and legs and read the corresponding sections.

12: Rebuilding Requires Periodic Renewal: Nehemiah 13

Purpose: To understand that revival isn't a one-time event but an ongoing lifestyle.

Question 2: The portion that was read was Deuteronomy 23:3–6. For background on this event, read Numbers 22—25.

Question 3: This is the same Tobiah who had opposed the rebuilding of the walls (2:10–19; 4:3, 7; 6:1, 12, 17, 19). Now he was living within them, a handy location for doing more harm.

Question 13: Note that Nehemiah didn't mention rebuilding the walls when he concluded his memoirs. Instead, his focus was on people.

Summary: If you have time, use these questions to summarize your study of Nehemiah: What kind of man was Nehemiah? What character qualities did Nehemiah possess that you'd like to emulate? What did you learn about God from this account of Nehemiah's life and work?

Conclusion: Play a recording of "Find Us Faithful," sung by Steve Green, or "Legacy," by Nicole Nordeman.

Endnotes

Session Nine
1. Charles G. Finney, *Lectures on Revivals of Religion: How to Promote a Revival* (*www.gospeltruth.net*).

Leaders Guide
1. Warren W. Wiersbe, *Be Determined*, Wheaton, Ill.: Victor Books, 1992, p. 87.

Bibliography

Brown, Raymond. *The Message of Nehemiah.* Downers Grove, Ill.: InterVarsity Press, 1998.

Kidner, Derek. *Ezra and Nehemiah.* Downers Grove, Ill.: InterVarsity Press, 1979.

Packer, J. I. *A Passion for Faithfulness: Wisdom from the Book of Nehemiah.* Wheaton, Ill.: Crossway Books, 1995.

Wiersbe, Warren W. *Be Determined.* Colorado Springs: Victor, 1992.